942.08

Contents

Clues about Queen Victoria   2

Public Buildings   4

Homes   6

Schools   8

Pictures of Places   12

Pictures of People   14

The Census   18

Maps and Sales Particulars   20

Victorian Objects   22

Newspapers   24

D0543155

MBC

Clues about Queen Victoria

Wherever you are in Britain, there are clues which can help you find out about the Victorians and their time. This book will help your investigations.

Start by looking for evidence of Queen Victoria and her family, like this postbox, which is one of the oldest in the country.

VR on the postbox stands for *Victoria Regina*. 'Regina' is the Latin word for 'Queen'. The first postage stamp was called the Penny Black and went on sale in 1840.

 More clues to look for:

Victorian postage stamps.
Look for Queen Victoria on British stamps and on stamps from countries which were once in the British Empire.

Victorian pennies.
Some show Victoria as a young woman; others show her as an old woman.

This statue of Queen Victoria is in London, but there are many others all over Britain. Some of them were put up at the time of the Queen's Golden Jubilee in 1887.

A lot of pubs were called the Queen Victoria or the Jubilee if they were built at that time. Perhaps there is one near where you live.

Many places were named after the Queen and her family, particularly her husband, Prince Albert. Are there any in your town or village?

VICTORIA AVENUE

JUBILEE PARK

ALBERT SQUARE

 More name clues to look for:

Streets, squares, parks, fountains, stations and bridges were named after the Queen. In the Empire, towns, states, mountains and waterfalls were named after the Queen. Find some of them on a map of the world.

Public Buildings

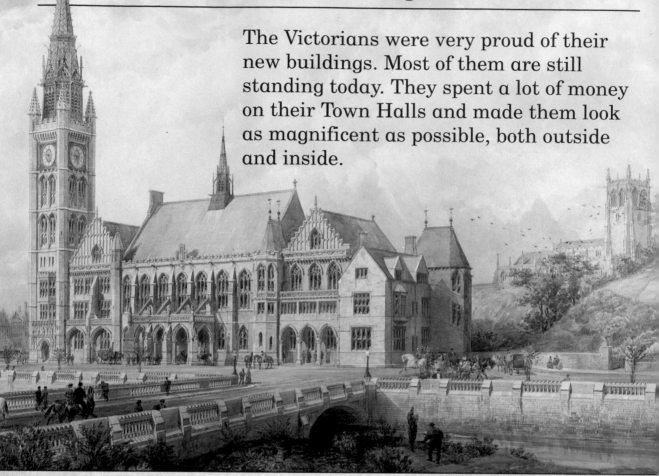

The Victorians were very proud of their new buildings. Most of them are still standing today. They spent a lot of money on their Town Halls and made them look as magnificent as possible, both outside and inside.

This is the Town Hall in Rochdale. When it was built in 1871, Rochdale was a centre for the cotton industry. The Town Hall cost £155,000 to build.

Inside the building there are stained glass windows, painted wall panels, stone carvings and angels painted in gold.

 More public buildings to look for:

Post offices, hospitals, schools, pumping stations, mills, factories, churches, banks, offices, law courts, prisons, theatres and concert halls. Some of them have foundation stones to tell you when they were opened.

The Railway

In Victorian times, people could travel by steam train to almost any town and village in Britain.

Big stations, like this one in Bristol, were designed by important architects. Many of them chose iron as a building material. Hundreds of passengers used this station every day. They still use it now.

Decorative iron pillars like these were used to hold up the roof in many stations. Gas or oil lights hung from the roof.

More railway clues to look for:

Railway bridges, level crossings, signal boxes, train sheds, pub signs, street names, railway hotels, houses where railway workers lived. Talk to older people with memories of travelling on a steam train.

In Victorian Britain, workers and their families lived in rows of small terraced houses like these. They were called 'two up, two down' houses, because they had two living rooms and two bedrooms.

Everyone burnt coal to keep the house warm, heat the water and cook the food. The families who live in the same houses today have put in central heating, new kitchens and bathrooms.

Why were there no garages next to Victorian houses?

Look for clues about life at home a hundred years ago.

More clues to look for:

Iron railings and coal hole covers, tiled paths to the front door, terrace names. Sometimes the builder used the names of famous people. Bootscrapers, where people took off the mud from their boots.

This painting shows a Victorian home built for a wealthy family. It was designed by a famous architect called William Burges, but you can find houses like it in many big cities. Look carefully at the picture.

- How many **storeys** did the house have? Rich people had a lot of servants.

- Which rooms had the largest windows — those at ground level or those at the top of the house? Servants lived in the rooms at the top.

- Find a window for the part of the house which was below the level of the street. The kitchen was usually in this part, called 'below stairs'.

- Which windows have coloured glass, called 'stained' glass, a bit like a church? What do you think the rooms were like inside?

Storeys

Floors.

 More clues to look for:

Blue plaques on the outside of houses, which tell us that someone famous once lived in the house.

Schools

The first Victorian schools were built in villages, near the church or chapel. By 1870, more people lived in the town than in the country. A new law said that committees, called School Boards, had to build schools in places where most children lived.

Board Schools, like the one in this photograph were built by School Boards in 1870.

There were so many children living in the towns that some Board Schools were very big. The infants were on the ground floor, the girls on the second floor and the boys at the top.

 More clues to look for:

Street names like School Lane. Architects' plans for the school when it was new. The plans are kept in the County Record Office.

Novr 16th Rev^d H Vaughan visited the School this morning. Ordinary Progress

17th Thomas Martin allowed to return to School again

18th Ordinary progress.

19th Children examined in Scripture.

20th Shorter School this week, several seem to be staying away for want of shoes to come in, instead of which they might be well provided with them by belonging to our Shoe Club. Average for the week 64

23rd Rather better School than last week, many of the bigger boys returned from work.

24th Admitted 3 fresh boys William Crossman Thomas Page and George Dawson.

25th I find the 4th Standard is progressing with Compound Division and Multiplication. Ordinary Progress in the other Standards.

26th Boys very noisy all day, they seemed to share in the general excitement occasioned by the Election.

27th To day the children had half a holiday in honour of Col Brise having achieved a great victory over the Liberals and become

A Victorian Log Book

An entry from a Log Book

Every day Victorian head teachers had to write in the School Log Book. Some Log Books are still kept in school cupboards, but others have been put into an **archive** for safe keeping. If your school was not built in Victorian times you can read a Log Book from another school in the County Record Office.

Log Books are full of information about life at school in the past. Teachers wrote about:

- the lessons and books they used;

- some of the children, particularly when they were late or naughty;

- the teachers and their wages;

- visitors to the school, especially the School Inspectors who came to give the children tests;

- illnesses and epidemics;

- concerts and special celebration days like Empire Day or the Queen's Golden Jubilee.

Archive

A special place where historic documents are kept.

Some archives have more documents about schools in Victorian times. They help us find out what has changed about school over the past hundred years and what is still the same.

Rough Inventory of Furniture
School Room

4 Desks 10·0 long convertible	2 Easles
2 Desks 8·0 long ditto	2 Boards
4 Desks 6·0 long ditto	2 Cupboards
3 Forms 7·0 long	5'0" × 8'0" × 1'0"
1 Mistress desk	1 Clock
1 Table	2 Small cases of specimens
3 Chairs	1 Terrestrial globe
1 Harmonium	3 Hanging lamps
2 Blackboards in frame on castors	3 Brackets lamps
	3 Window blinds
	1 Curtain over door

This list of things, in a school built in 1872, was made when the County Council took it over in 1903. The school only had two classrooms. Can you use the list to decide what the classrooms looked like inside and what some of the lessons were about?

Harmonium	**Terrestrial Globe**
A musical instrument.	A globe of the earth.

More document clues to look for:

Registers, punishment books and books used by children learning to read and write.

The first school photographs were taken in the 1880s.
Most children had never seen a camera before.

These children went to St Peter's School in Macclesfield.

It was a church school and the photograph was
taken outside the church door.

- How old do you think the children were?

- What were their school clothes like?

- Where are the teachers?

- Where is the parish priest? Why was he in the
  photograph?

- What do you think about the expressions on the
  children's faces? Some people were frightened
  of a camera if they had not seen one before.

 **More school
clues to look
for:**

Badges, certificates,
cups, shields, school
uniform, slates,
counting frames,
globes and charts.

Pictures of Places

Drawing and painting was a popular occupation in Victorian times. An artist called Louise Rayner painted this picture of Cambridge in 1881. Some of the buildings look the same today, but the scene in the street has changed a lot.

Find:

- the man riding a horse. Today people ride bicycles down this street.

- horse-drawn carriages. Today the street is full of cars.

- rails in the middle of the street. This was for the horse-drawn tram. Today there are buses and taxis.

- children playing with a hoop. The street is too busy to play in today.

- people dressed in Victorian clothes.

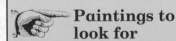 **Paintings to look for**

Victorian paintings can be found in art galleries, museums and even people's houses.

The invention of photography in Victorian times means that they left behind lots of photographs of themselves and where they lived.

This photograph was taken in 1880 in the same town as the painting on page 12.

Find:

- a butcher's shop.
- a street light which worked by gas.
- market stalls.
- horse-drawn vehicles.
- people looking at the camera.

 Old and new clues to look for:

Find an old photograph of your town or village and take a picture of the same view today. How many things have changed?

We can recognise Victorian photographs because they are either a 'sepia', or brown colour, or they are black and white.

This photograph was taken to show well-off people how poor children lived. The girl on the right of the picture moved when the photo was being taken, so we cannot see her face properly.

Local libraries collect old photographs of people who once lived in their locality. Even when they do not know who the people were, the photographs tell us a lot about Victorian times — such as what people wore, where they lived, what work they did and how they enjoyed themselves.

The women and children in this photograph worked for a basket maker. You can see him on the left-hand side of the picture. They had to strip the bark off twigs which were then woven into baskets.

 Group photographs to look for:

People who lived in the same street.
People at work or on holiday.

Family Albums

Some grannies and grandads have an album with photographs of their grannies and grandads. Cameras and film were too expensive for ordinary families to buy. A photographer took their photos on special occasions like weddings.

The photographer has arranged this wedding group very carefully for the photo.

Find:

- the bride and bridegroom with their families.

- the hats. The round bowler hats were worn by the men. The big hats decorated with flowers were worn by the women.

What was the smart fashion for boys? for babies?

Do you think people in the past had larger or smaller families than they have today?

Some family photographs were taken in a studio, which was decorated with curtains, plants and objects. The people in the photographs were arranged like a scene in a play or film.

Look at the inside of this photographer's studio. The woman wore her best dress for the photo. Under the dress she wore a corset which was tightened with laces to make her waist look small.

SCARBOROUGH.

GUNN & STUART   RICHMOND
                         SURREY

This is another studio photograph. The photographer has put ferns and furs in the studio. The boys are wearing sailor suits which were fashionable in the second half of Victoria's reign.

 More clues to look for :

The photographer's name on the bottom or the back of a studio photograph. Use street directories in your local library to find out where the studio was.

The Census

Every ten years a national census is taken. Everyone in Great Britain is counted on the same night. We fill in our own census forms, but in Victorian times a census **enumerator** called at every house.

Anne Orbiston Ellen Price Annie Jane Harrop Emily Jackson Dan Chapman

Edward Stockbridge

Eliza Turtlebury

John Fordham

Edward Fordham

Miss Lawson

Alfred Fordham

Mrs Catherine Fordham

This photograph was taken of the Fordham household on census night, 21 April 1891.

Enumerator
A person who went from house to house and filled in the census forms.

Name of Road, Street or House
Melbourne Bury
Melbourne Bury
Melbourne Bury
Melbourne Bury
Melbourne Bury
Melbourne Bury
Melbourne Bury
Melbourne Bury
Melbourne Bury
Melbourne Bury
Melbourne Bury
Melbourne Bury

This is the actual
census form from 1891.

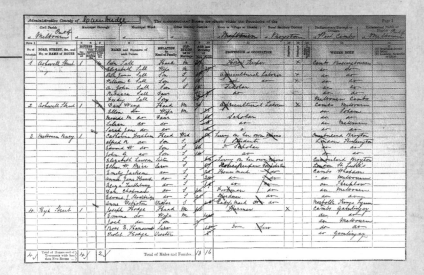

This is what the actual census form said. It shows :

- the names of everyone living in the house on census night.

- their ages.

- their relationship to the head of the house. The head of this household is Mrs Fordham, a widow.

- their job or if they had enough money without taking a job.

- any 'scholars' or people who went to school.

- the place where they were born.

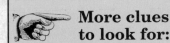

More clues to look for:

Census returns for your locality.
Street directories with names and jobs of householders.

Name and surname of each person	Relation to Head of Family	Condition as to marriage	Age last birthday	Profession or Occupation	Where born
Catherine Fordham	Head	Widow	52	Living on her own income	Cumberland, Broyton
Alfred Fordham	Son	Single	18	Student	London, Kensington
Edward W. Fordham	Son	Single	16	Scholar	London, Kensington
John G. Fordham	Son	Single	14	Scholar	London, Kensington
Elizabeth Lawson	Sister	Single	64	Living on her own income	Cumberland, Broyton
Ellen W. Price	Servant	Single	57	Housekeeper and domestic	London, St Luke's
Emily Jackson	Servant	Single	20	Housemaid and domestic	Cambs, Whaddon
Annie Jane Harrop	Servant	Single	24	Housemaid and domestic	Cambs, Melbourne
Elizabeth Turtlebury	Servant	Single	19	Housemaid and domestic	Cambs, Thriplow
John Chapman	Servant	Single	24	Footman	Cambs, Melbourne
Edward J. Stockbridge	Servant	Single	25	Gardener	Cambs, Melbourne
Anne Orbiston	Visitor	Single	46	Lady's Maid	Norfolk, King's Lynn

Perhaps you live in a place where most of the streets and houses were built in the twentieth century, not in Victorian times. You will have to use an old map to find out what was there a hundred years ago.

The Manor School in this photograph was built in 1959.

This map was drawn in 1901 and shows us what was there before.

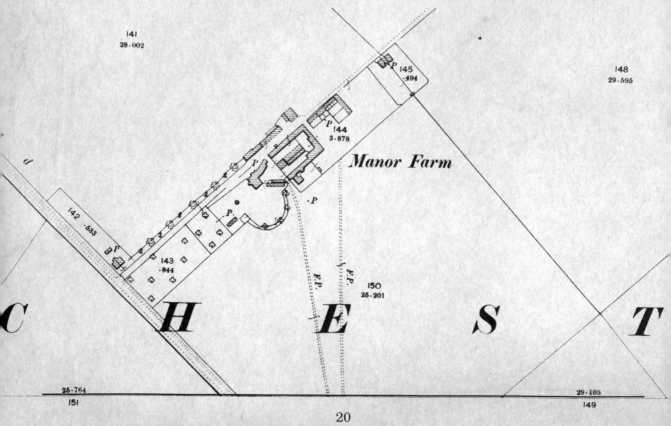

Lot 3.

(Edged Pink on plan.)

THE VERY SUPERIOR

Attractive Freehold Farm

with possession on 11th October, 1909, Land Tax redeemed, and known as

"The Manor Farm"

comprising a well-constructed brick built and tiled

FAMILY RESIDENCE

approached from the Arbury Road by a

- - Carriage Drive - -

has the following accommodation

On Ground Floor:—which is lofty and well-lighted, ENTRANCE LOBBY, with coloured glass panels to door and window, HALL 7 feet wide. DINING ROOM about 19 ft. by 14 ft. 6 in., including Bay Window, with polished Slate Mantel, Modern Stove and Tiled Hearth, and Inside Shutters. DRAWING ROOM about 19 ft. by 14 ft. 3 in., including Bay Window, with Marble Mantle, Modern Grate, and Tiled Hearth and Inside Shutters. STUDY. MORNING ROOM with Modern Grate and Tiled Hearth. KITCHEN, having Range fitted with high pressure boiler. Two Pantries, BACK KITCHEN with Brick Oven, and Sink, Coal House with Smoke Room.

On First Floor:—which is approached by Front and Back Stairways, LANDING, BEDROOM over Dining Room about 15 ft. 9 in. by 14 ft. 5 in., with two windows. BEDROOM over Drawing Room, about 15 ft. 9 in. by 14 ft. 3 in. DRESSING ROOM, BEDROOM over Sudy, BEDROOM over Morning Room and SERVANTS' BEDROOM, BATHROOM with Hot Water Supply and W.C.

Second Floor:—TWO BEDROOMS.

In Basement, which has a separate Area Entrance, COOL DAIRY and CELLAR.

A POULTRY YARD

on the South East of the House separates it from the Homestead, and contains three Brick, Timber, and Tiled Fowlhouses and Potting Shed, and a small Paved Yard, with 2 W.C's.

(Lot 3 continued).

A central range of brick, timber and tiled Buildings embraces a

COW HOUSE FOR 20 COWS

6 loose boxes and a

7 Bay Open Shed.

Adjoining the Chaisehouse is a brick, timber and tiled

9 BAY CART LODGE,

near to is a timber and tiled engine and machine Shed with a lean-to Workshop.

THE SECOND FARM YARD.

On the North West:—An 8 Bay open Shed, 2 loose Boxes and several pigstyes all timber built and roofed with corrugated iron.

On the North East:—An 8 Bay open Shed; together with

Five Stockyards.

Adjoining the Homestead is an

ENCLOSED STACKYARD.

THE FOREMAN'S HOUSE

adjoins the first Farmyard, is built of brick, with tiled roof, and contains

On Ground Floor:—Two Sitting Rooms, Kitchen with Sink, and Pantry.

On Upper Floor:—Three Bedrooms; surrounding the House is a

Walled-in Garden.

Beyond the Stackyard are

TWO BRICK & TILED COTTAGES

with LARGE GARDENS; each containing

On Ground Floor:—Sitting Room, Kitchen, and Pantry.

On Upper Floor:—Three Bedrooms. Between these Cottages and forming part of the Ground Floor is a

General Labourers' Mess Room.

The farmhouse was pulled down before the school was built. We can find out more about it from this old photograph and advertisement for the farm when it was sold.

 More clues:

The census tells us who lived at Manor farm, some people can still remember what it looked like and who lived there.

Victorian Objects

Lots of people collect things which were made and used in Victorian times.

Objects help us to find out:

- the materials, like iron, wood, tin, wool and cotton, which the Victorians used to make things.

- things they used at work, at home and at school.

- designs they liked.

We can find out about housework a hundred years ago from looking at the things people used to do the washing.

This is a model of a Victorian slate.

We can find out about life at school from an old slate or book.

This wooden bobbin was once part of a machine in a woollen factory.

Museums collect old objects, keep them in good repair and put them on display. Your local museum will have things used by people who lived in your town or village.

At this museum, all the objects have been put into an old cottage. Someone alive today has dressed up to pretend to be Victorian.

Other museums like this have been opened at old coal mines, factories, docks and schools. They all help us to discover what life was like for the people who lived there a hundred years ago.

 More objects to look for:

Clothes worn in Victorian times.
Victorian furniture.
Mugs and plates with pictures of Queen Victoria.

Local newspapers are another good source for finding out about your area in Victorian times. Ask for copies in your local library. The advertisements will tell you what people could buy or what jobs were available.

This newspaper was started in 1861.
It is still sold today, but it is now called the Lancashire Evening News.

 Newspaper clues to look for:

The Illustrated London News for national events.
Your local newspaper in the library or County Record Office.